Dallas WINGS

by Luke Hanlon

Copyright © 2026 by Press Room Editions. All rights reserved. No part of this book may be used or reproduced in any manner whatsoever, including internet usage, without written permission from the copyright owner, except in the case of brief quotations embodied in critical articles and reviews.

Book design by Kate Liestman
Cover design by Kate Liestman

Photographs ©: Erica Denhoff/Icon Sportswire/AP Images, cover; Cooper Neill/Getty Images Sport/Getty Images, 4, 7, 8; Carlos Osorio/AP Images, 10; Eliot J. Schechter/Allsport/Getty Images Sport/Getty Images, 13; Richard Carson/AP Images, 15; Tom Pidgeon/Getty Images Sport/Getty Images, 16, 19; Gregory Shamus/Getty Images Sport/Getty Images, 20, 23; Tim Clayton/Corbis Sport/Getty Images, 24, 27; Quinn Harris/Getty Images Sport/Getty Images, 28

Press Box Books, an imprint of Press Room Editions.

ISBN
979-8-89469-012-4 (library bound)
979-8-89469-025-4 (paperback)
979-8-89469-050-6 (epub)
979-8-89469-038-4 (hosted ebook)

Library of Congress Control Number: 2025930749

Distributed by North Star Editions, Inc.
2297 Waters Drive
Mendota Heights, MN 55120
www.northstareditions.com

Printed in the United States of America
082025

ABOUT THE AUTHOR

Luke Hanlon is a sportswriter and editor based in Minneapolis. He's written dozens of nonfiction sports books for kids and spends a lot of his free time watching his favorite Minnesota sports teams.

TABLE OF CONTENTS

CHAPTER 1
SCORING MACHINE   5

CHAPTER 2
GROWING PAINS   11

CHAPTER 3
SHOCK FORCE   17

SUPERSTAR PROFILE
DEANNA NOLAN   22

CHAPTER 4
ON THE MOVE   25

QUICK STATS   30
GLOSSARY   31
TO LEARN MORE   32
INDEX   32

CHAPTER 1

SCORING MACHINE

Arike Ogunbowale received a pass. She was standing well beyond the three-point arc. A defender ran out to guard her. But she wasn't quick enough. Ogunbowale released a deep three-pointer. The ball hit nothing but net.

Ogunbowale's shot gave the Dallas Wings a seven-point lead early in the

---

Arike Ogunbowale averaged 22.2 points per game in 2024.

fourth quarter. The Wings were playing the Phoenix Mercury during the 2024 Women's National Basketball Association (WNBA) season. Dallas had led by 24 points in the third quarter. However, the Mercury fought back. They came within four points of the Wings. Then Ogunbowale took over.

About three minutes later, Ogunbowale drove hard to her right. She blew past a Phoenix defender and banked in a shot. A few possessions later, a defender forced Ogunbowale to drive to her left. She then rose up for a shot. The defender's hand was right in Ogunbowale's face. But the tough defense didn't faze her. The shot still fell through the basket. Ogunbowale

Ogunbowale dribbles past a Mercury defender in a 2024 game.

then stared down some courtside Mercury fans.

Ogunbowale was locked in. Every player on the floor knew it. On the next possession, Ogunbowale raised her hand as she crossed half-court. A teammate passed to her. A defender met her

Ogunbowale (24) scored 30 or more points in a game six times in 2024.

right away. Ogunbowale dribbled hard to her left. Then she chucked a deep shot. The crowd in Phoenix groaned as the ball went in.

Late in the fourth quarter, the Wings led by 15. But Ogunbowale kept pushing. She faked a shot near the three-point line.

Then she glided by a defender. Another came to stop her. So, Ogunbowale leaned to her left. She put up an off-balance shot. It banked in off the backboard.

Ogunbowale scored 19 points in the fourth quarter. She finished the game with 40 points. Her scoring led the Wings to a comfortable win. Dallas fans had gotten used to performances like this from their star guard. And they hoped there would be many more to come.

NOTHING NEW

Arike Ogunbowale entered the WNBA in 2019. Over the next six years, few players scored as easily as she did. Going into 2025, Ogunbowale averaged at least 18 points per game every season. In 2020, she averaged 22.8 points per game. She led the league in scoring that year.

CHAPTER 2

GROWING PAINS

The history of the Dallas Wings started in 1998. The WNBA was coming off a successful first season. So, the league decided to add two new teams. Neither team played in Dallas, though. The Wings started as the Detroit Shock.

Detroit hired Nancy Lieberman as the team's coach and general

Nancy Lieberman had no previous coaching experience when the Shock hired her in 1998.

manager. Lieberman had enjoyed a legendary playing career. She'd earned a spot in the Basketball Hall of Fame. The Shock hoped Lieberman would have similar success building a team.

However, the Shock got off to a rough start. They lost their first four games of the 1998 season. Even so, Lieberman rallied the team. Detroit finished with a 17–13 record. The Shock just missed out on a playoff spot.

A LEGEND RETURNS

Lynette Woodard left the University of Kansas in 1981. At the time, she was the leading scorer in women's college basketball history. Woodard came out of retirement in 1997 when the WNBA started. In 1998, she joined the Shock for her final season. At the age of 38, Woodard averaged 3.5 points per game with Detroit.

Jennifer Azzi averaged 10.8 points per game in 1999, her only year with Detroit.

In 1999, Lieberman led the Shock to playoffs. However, they lost in the first round. Then in 2000, the team finished with a losing record. After the season ended, Detroit fired Lieberman.

The Shock hired Greg Williams as their new coach before the 2001 season. The decision didn't work out, though. Detroit tied for the worst record in the WNBA that year. Then in 2002, the Shock started the season 0–10. The team quickly fired Williams and hired Bill Laimbeer.

Basketball fans in Detroit already loved Laimbeer. He had won two National Basketball Association (NBA) titles as a player for the Detroit Pistons. He brought that winning attitude to the Shock.

In his playing days, Laimbeer was known for being tough. He wanted the Shock to play the same way. The team improved on offense and defense under Laimbeer. Detroit went 9–13 to finish the

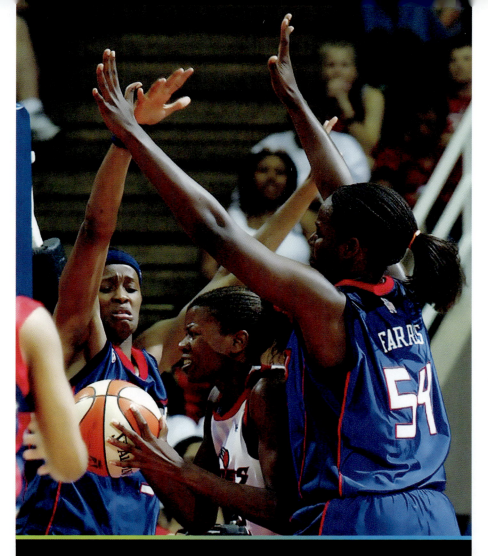

Shock players swarm an opposing player during a 2002 game.

2002 season. The Shock were still at the bottom of the standings. But they were heading in the right direction.

CHAPTER 3

SHOCK FORCE

The years of losing provided one benefit for the Shock. Teams with bad records have a better chance of getting high draft picks. Each year from 2001 to 2003, the Shock selected in the top six of the draft. They picked Deanna Nolan, Swin Cash, and Cheryl Ford. Detroit finally looked ready to compete.

Deanna Nolan averaged 12.4 points per game in 2003.

Bill Laimbeer turned that core of players into a dominant team. The Shock finished the 2003 season with the league's best record. They lost only one playoff game on their way to the WNBA Finals.

Detroit faced the Los Angeles Sparks in the Finals. Los Angeles was the two-time defending champion. But the Shock didn't back down. The teams split the first two games of the series. That set up a winner-take-all Game 3 in Detroit. Ford made two clutch free throws with 12 seconds left to seal the win. A record crowd of 22,076 fans erupted after the final buzzer. They celebrated the Shock's first championship.

Cheryl Ford (35) shoots over two Los Angeles Sparks defenders in the 2003 Finals.

The Shock made the playoffs again in 2004. However, they lost in the first round. Then the team made a big move in the middle of the 2005 season. Detroit traded for Katie Smith. The veteran guard

19

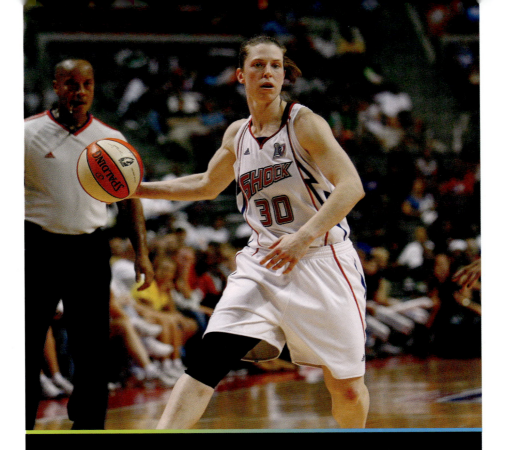

Katie Smith made two All-Star teams while she played with the Shock.

provided more scoring for the Shock. Even so, they lost in the first round of the playoffs again.

In 2006, Smith combined with the Shock's core players perfectly. The team made it back to the Finals. The series was now the best of five games. Nolan scored 24 points at home in Game 5. Her scoring led the Shock to another title.

Laimbeer kept the Shock rolling after that. They made it back to the Finals in 2007 and 2008. They lost in 2007. But the Shock won the title in front of their home crowd in 2008. Six years earlier, they'd been the WNBA's worst team. Now Detroit had become a dynasty.

MAKING MORE HISTORY

Nancy Lieberman returned to the Detroit Shock in 2008. But it wasn't to coach or to be the general manager. She came back to play. Bill Laimbeer signed her to a seven-day contract during the 2008 season. At 50 years old, Lieberman played in one game with the Shock. She broke her own record as the oldest player in WNBA history.

SUPERSTAR PROFILE

DEANNA NOLAN

Deanna Nolan grew up 70 miles (113 km) away from Detroit. The Shock drafted her in 2001. She proved to be a key player for Detroit over the next nine seasons.

Nolan was a complete player. She used her quickness to zoom past defenders. She could lock down opponents with her defense, too. And she always stepped up in the biggest moments. Nolan hit two late free throws in Game 2 of the 2003 Finals. Those points saved Detroit's season. Then she hit a three-pointer to give the Shock the lead late in Game 3. That shot helped secure Detroit's first title.

Nolan played even better in the 2006 Finals. She averaged 17.8 points per game in that series. Nolan won the Finals Most Valuable Player (MVP) Award for her performance.

Nolan made the All-WNBA First Team twice in her career.

CHAPTER 4

ON THE MOVE

The good times in Detroit didn't last. Early in the 2009 season, Bill Laimbeer left the team. Also, the Shock were losing money. New owners bought the team after the 2009 season. They moved the Shock from Detroit to Tulsa, Oklahoma.

Deanna Nolan, Cheryl Ford, and Katie Smith had all played with Detroit

The Tulsa Shock selected Skylar Diggins-Smith third overall in the 2013 draft.

in 2009. But none of them played with Tulsa. The lack of talent showed on the court. The Shock had losing records in their first five seasons in Tulsa. In 2015, the team's owner announced that the Shock would leave Tulsa when the season ended.

Before the 2016 season, the Tulsa Shock became the Dallas Wings. All-Star guard Skylar Diggins-Smith made the move to Texas with the Wings. Then Dallas selected guard Allisha Gray in the 2017 draft. The rookie clicked right away with Diggins-Smith. That duo helped the Wings reach the playoffs in 2017 and 2018. However, they lost in the first round each time.

Allisha Gray (15) won the WNBA Rookie of the Year Award in 2017.

Diggins-Smith never played for the Wings again after the 2018 season. But the team reloaded in the 2019 draft. The Wings selected Arike Ogunbowale with the fifth pick. The guard could score from almost anywhere on the court. Then, in

Satou Sabally made her second career All-Star team in 2023.

the 2020 draft, Dallas added another talented scorer in forward Satou Sabally.

Ogunbowale and Sabally led the Wings back to the playoffs in 2021 and 2022. Dallas couldn't get past the first round in either of those years. But the Wings came back stronger in 2023. Sabally scored 32 points in the first game of the playoffs that year. Ogunbowale added 24 to help the Wings win. Then Dallas won Game 2 to sweep the series. For the first time since leaving Detroit, the team had won a playoff series.

Sabally left Dallas after the 2024 season. So, the team continued to build around Ogunbowale. Fans believed she could lift the Wings to a title.

BEST OF THE BEST

During Olympic years, the WNBA All-Star Game features a game between All-Stars from the league and the US women's basketball team. Arike Ogunbowale didn't make the US team in 2021 or 2024. In both of those years, she led the All-Star team to victory and earned MVP honors.

QUICK STATS

DALLAS WINGS

Team history: Detroit Shock (1998–2009), Tulsa Shock (2010–15), Dallas Wings (2016–)

Championships: 3 (2003, 2006, 2008)

Key coaches:
- Nancy Lieberman (1998–2000): 46–48, 0–1 playoffs
- Bill Laimbeer (2002–09): 137–92, 27–16 playoffs, 3 WNBA titles
- Vickie Johnson (2021–22): 32–36, 1–3 playoffs

Most career points: Arike Ogunbowale (4,014)

Most career assists: Deanna Nolan (930)

Most career rebounds: Cheryl Ford (1,907)

Most career blocks: Ruth Riley (206)

Most career steals: Deanna Nolan (388)

Stats are accurate through the 2024 season.

GLOSSARY

clutch
Having to do with a difficult situation when the outcome of the game is in question.

contract
A written agreement that keeps a player with a team for a certain amount of time.

draft
An event that allows teams to choose new players coming into the league.

dynasty
A team that has an extended period of success, usually winning multiple championships in the process.

general manager
The person in a team's front office who drafts and signs new players.

rookie
A first-year player.

sweep
To win all the games in a series.

veteran
A player who has spent several years in a league.

TO LEARN MORE

Nicks, Erin. *Arike Ogunbowale*. Focus Readers, 2022.
O'Neal, Ciara. *The WNBA Finals*. Apex Editions, 2023.
Whiting, Jim. *The Story of the Dallas Wings*. Creative Education, 2024.

MORE INFORMATION

To learn more about the Dallas Wings, go to **pressboxbooks.com/AllAccess**. These links are routinely monitored and updated to provide the most current information available.

INDEX

Cash, Swin, 17

Detroit Pistons, 14
Diggins-Smith, Skylar, 26–27

Ford, Cheryl, 17–18, 25

Gray, Allisha, 26

Laimbeer, Bill, 14, 18, 21, 25
Lieberman, Nancy, 11–13, 21
Los Angeles Sparks, 18

Nolan, Deanna, 17, 21, 22, 25

Ogunbowale, Arike, 5–9, 27–29

Phoenix Mercury, 6–8

Sabally, Satou, 28–29
Smith, Katie, 19–20, 25

Williams, Greg, 14
Woodard, Lynette, 12